FIRST dictionary

make believe ideas

Aa

ambulance

An **ambulance** is a special van that takes people to hospital when they are hurt or sick.

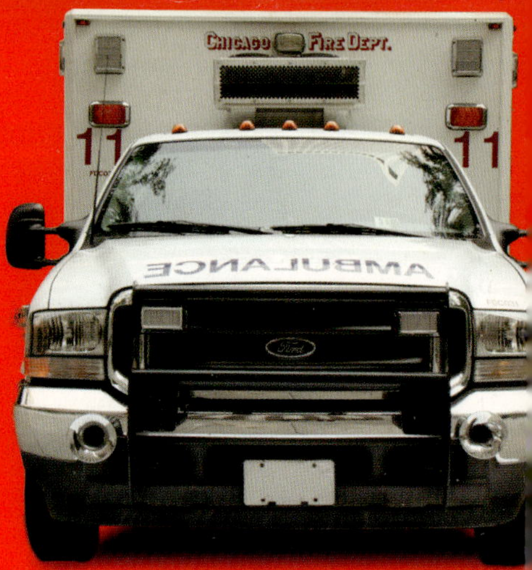

airplane

An **airplane** is a flying machine with wings that carries people and things.

angry

If you are **angry**, you feel very upset and annoyed.

animal

An **animal** is a livin thing that moves around. A plant is not an animal. Cats, chickens, spiders, and goldfish are all animals.

alphabet

An **alphabet** is a collection of letters used in writing, arranged in a special order.

apple

An **apple** is a round juicy fruit that grows on a tree. Its skin ca be green, red, or yellow.

Bb

bat

A **bat** is a piece of wood that is used to hit a ball in a game.

bed

A **bed** is something you lie down and sleep on.

ball

A **ball** is a round object used in games. You can throw, hit, catch, roll, or kick a ball.

bicycle

A **bicycle** is a machine you ride. It has two wheels and pedals.

banana

A **banana** is a long fruit with a thick, yellow skin.

bee

A **bee** is an insect with wings. Bees make honey.

bird

A **bird** is an animal with wings, feathers, and a beak. Most birds can fly.

basket

A **basket** is a container used to store or carry things.

beetle

A **beetle** is an insect that has hard, shiny wing covers.

body

The **body** of a person or an animal is every part of them.

book

A **book** is made up of lots of pages held together inside a cover.

bottle

A **bottle** holds liquid. It is usually made of glass or plastic.

bowl

A **bowl** is a deep dish that holds food like soup, breakfast cereal, or fruit.

box

A **box** is used to keep things in. Most boxes are made of plastic or cardboard.

boy

A **boy** is a child who will grow up to be a man.

bread

Bread is a food mac with flour. It is baked in an oven.

broccoli

Broccoli is a green vegetable.

brush

A **brush** has lots of stiff hairs or wires and usually has a handle.

bucket

A **bucket** is used to carry things like liquids or sand.

bulldozer

A **bulldozer** is a big machine with a shovel hat pushes rocks out of the way.

bus

A **bus** is a long vehicle with seats inside to carry people around.

button

A **button** is a small object that fastens clothes together.

butterfly

A **butterfly** is an insect that has large, colorful wings.

Cc

cake

A **cake** is a sweet food. It is made by mixing butter, sugar, eggs, and flour and baking it in an oven.

car

A **car** is a machine with four wheels and an engine that we use to get from one place to another.

A B C D E F G H I J K L M N O P Q R S T U V W X Y Z

carrot

A **carrot** is a long, orange vegetable that grows under the ground.

cat

A **cat** is an animal with soft fur, sharp claws, and a long tail. People keep small cats as pets.

catch

When you **catch** something, you take hold of it while it is moving.

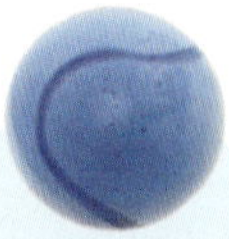

caterpillar

A **caterpillar** looks like a worm with legs. It turns into a butterfly or a moth.

chair

A **chair** is a seat with four legs and a back.

cheese

Cheese is a food made from milk.

child

A **child** is a young boy or girl. When there is more than one child, they are called children.

chocolate

Chocolate is a sweet food made from cocoa beans.

clock

A **clock** is a machine that shows you what time it is.

clown

A **clown** is someone who says and does funny things to make people laugh.

clothes

Clothes are the things that people wear, such as pants, dresses, and shirts.

color

Red, blue, and yellow are **colors**. By mixing them together, you get other colors.

computer

A **computer** is a machine that stores information and helps people to work.

comb

A **comb** is a piece of plastic or metal that has lots of thin teeth. You use a comb to fix your hair.

cow

A **cow** is a large female farm animal that produces milk. The male animal is called a bull and the baby is a calf.

crown

A **crown** is a kind of hat, usually worn by kings and queens. It is often made of gold or silver.

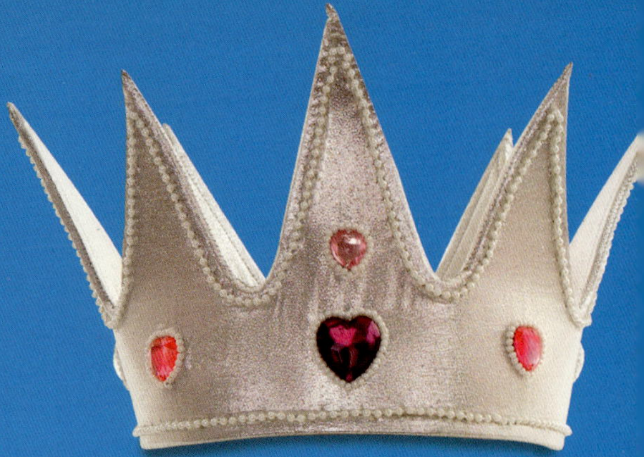

crawl

When you **crawl**, you move around on your hands and knees.

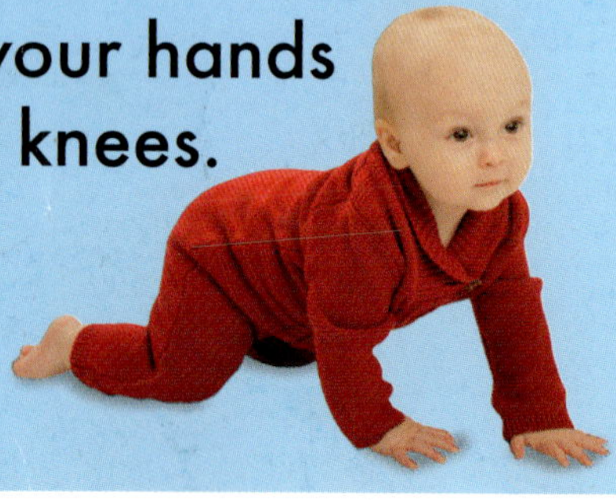

cry

When you **cry**, tears fall from your eyes.

cucumber

A **cucumber** is a long, green vegetable.

cup

A **cup** is a small, round container with a handle. You drink from a cup.

crocodile

A **crocodile** is an animal with sharp teeth, short legs, and a long tail.

Dd

doctor

A **doctor** takes care of people who are sick or hurt and helps them to get better.

dice

Dice are small cubes that have a different number of spots on each side.

dinosaur

Dinosaurs were animals that lived on Earth millions of years ago.

dish

A **dish** is a bowl for serving food.

dog

A **dog** is an animal that barks. Dogs are often kept as pets.

donkey

A **donkey** is a furry animal that looks like a small horse with long ears.

Ee

elephant

An **elephant** is a large, gray animal that has tusks, big ears, and a long nose called a trunk.

eagle

An **eagle** is a large bird with big wings, a curved beak, and sharp claws.

ear

Your **ears** are on each side of your head. You hear with your ears.

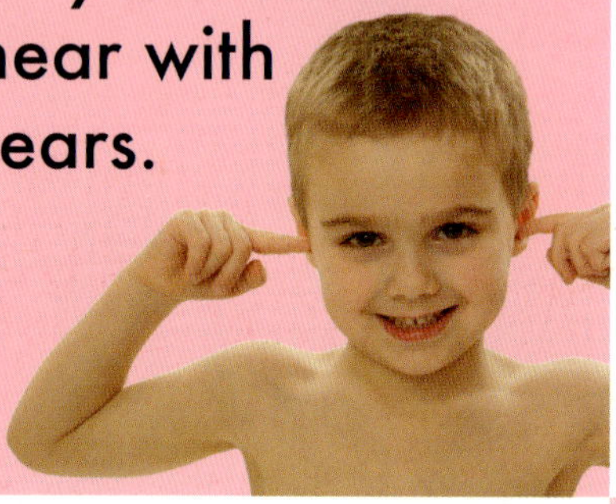

envelope

An **envelope** is a paper cover to put letters or cards inside.

eye

Your **eyes** are on your face. You see with your eyes.

egg

Many animals, such as birds, lizards, and some fish live inside **eggs** until they are big enough to hatch out.

exercise

When you **exercise**, you move your body to keep fit.

Ff

face

Your **face** is the front part of your head. Your eyes, nose, and mouth are all part of your face.

farm

A **farm** is a place where farmers grow food and raise animals.

family

Your **family** is the group of people that are closest to you. Your mom, dad, brothers, and sisters are all part of your family.

feather

Birds have **feathers** on their bodies to keep them warm and dry. Feathers also help birds fly.

finger

Your **fingers** are part of your hand. Each hand has four fingers and a thumb.

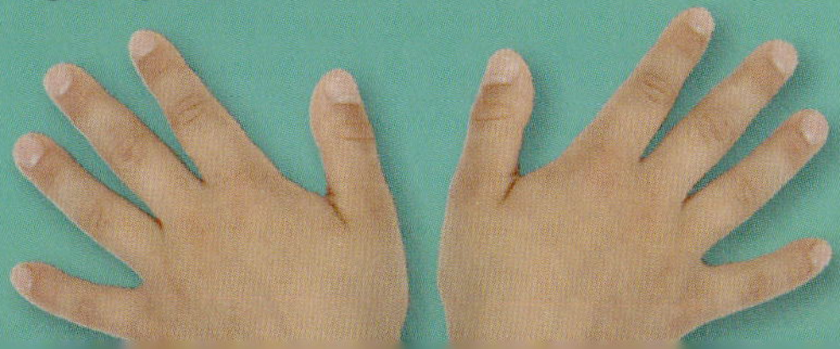

fire

A **fire** is the hot, bright flames and smoke made when something is burning.

fire truck

A **fire truck** is a vehicle with a ladder and a water hose. Firefighters use fire trucks to drive to fires and put them out.

fish

A **fish** is an animal that lives in water. Fish have fins to swim and gills to "breathe" underwater.

flower

A **flower** is part of a plant. Many flowers smell nice and are bright colors.

food

Food is what you eat to keep you strong and healthy.

fork

A **fork** has sharp prongs and a handle. You use a small fork for eating and a big fork for digging in the garden.

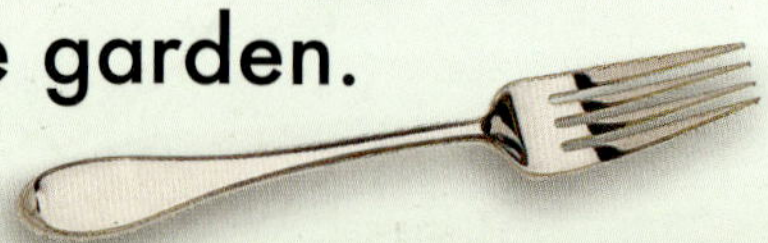

frog

A **frog** is a small animal that lives in damp places.

fruit

A **fruit** is the part of a plant that holds the seeds. Lots of fruits, such as apples and grapes, are juicy and good to eat.

Gg

giraffe

A **giraffe** is a tall animal with long legs and a very long neck.

goat

A **goat** is an animal with long hair and horns on its head.

game

A **game** is what you play for fun. Bat and ball is a game.

gate

A **gate** is a kind of door in a wall, fence, or hedge.

grape

A **grape** is a small purple or green fruit that grows in bunches. Grapes are used to make wine.

girl

A **girl** is a child who will grow up to be a woman.

grow

When somebody or something **grows**, it gets bigger.

Hh

helicopter

A **helicopter** is a flying machine with blades that spin instead of wings. The blades allow it to lift up straight from the ground and hover.

half

A **half** is one of two pieces that are equal in size.

hop

You **hop** when you jump up and down on one leg.

house

A **house** is a buildin where people eat, sleep, and live. Houses have roofs, walls, doors, and windows to keep the people inside warm and dry.

hammer

A **hammer** is a tool you can use to hit nails into wood.

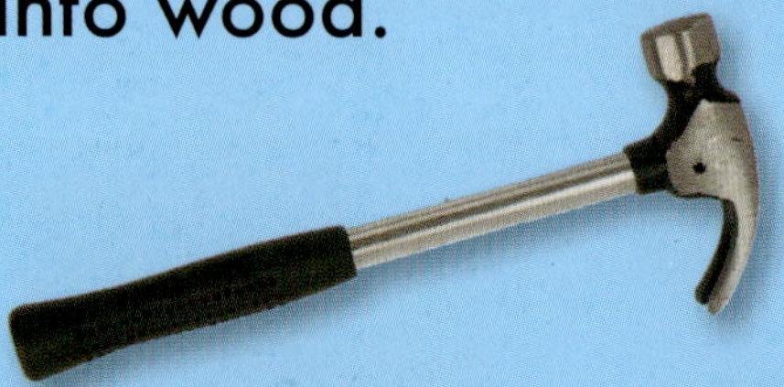

head

Your **head** is the part of your body that is above your neck.

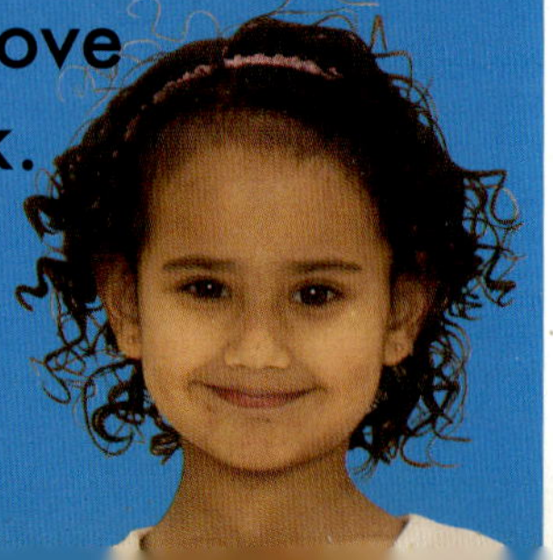

horse

A **horse** is a big animal with hooves. People ride horses and use them to pull heavy loads.

Ii

idea

An **idea** is a thought you have about something.

ice

Ice is made when water freezes. It is very cold and hard.

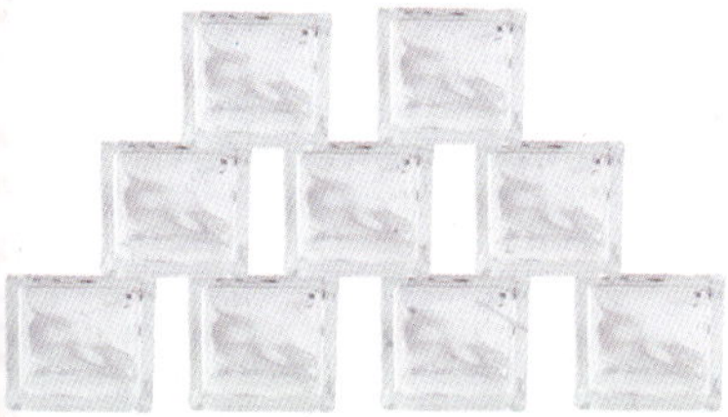

ice cream

Ice cream is a sweet, creamy, frozen food.

insects

An **insect** is a small animal with six legs. Many insects have wings. Ants, beetles, butterflies, and bees are all insects.

Jj

jar

Jars are usually made of glass. They close tightly and keep foods, like jelly, fresh.

jewel

A **jewel** is a beautiful, sparkling stone. Some jewels, like diamonds, cost a lot of money.

a b c d e f g h i j k l m n o p q r s t u v w x y z

A B C D E F G H I J K L M N O P Q R S T U V W X Y Z

Kk

jigsaw puzzle

A **jigsaw puzzle** is made from lots of pieces that fit together to make a picture.

kid

A **kid** is the name for a baby goat. Children can also be called kids.

juice

Juice is the liquid that comes out of a fruit when you squeeze it.

key

A **key** is a specially shaped piece of metal that is used to lock or unlock a door.

king

A **king** is a man who is born to rule a country.

jump

When you **jump**, you push both feet off the ground and move suddenly up into the air.

kick

When you **kick** something, you hit it with your foot.

knife

A **knife** is a tool used for cutting. Mos knives have a handle and a long, sharp, metal blade.

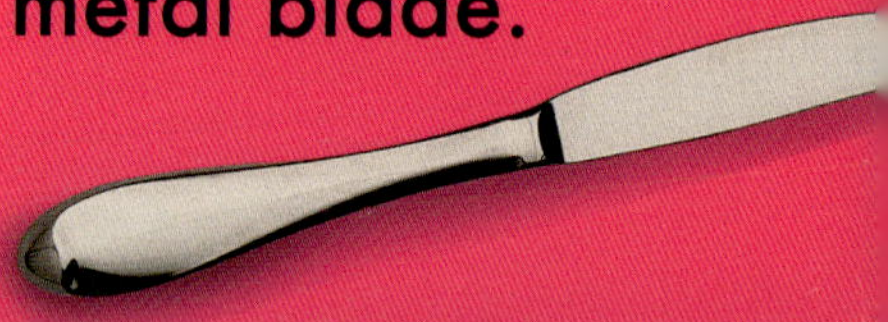

Ll

adder

You use a **ladder** o climb up high. Ladders are made of metal or wood.

amb

A **lamb** is a young sheep that is still with its mother.

lamp

A **lamp** gives you light. You can move a lamp around and switch it on and off.

leaf

A **leaf** is one of the flat, green parts of a plant or tree.

lemon

A **lemon** is a juicy, yellow fruit with a sour taste.

letter

A **letter** is a sign you use to write words. A, m, and z are all letters. A letter is also what you can write to a friend or relative.

lion

A **lion** is a big, wild cat. Lions live in Africa and India.

Mm

mask

A **mask** is something that you wear to cover your face. People wear masks to change the way they look.

man

A **man** is a grown-up male person.

medicine

You take **medicine** when you are sick in order to make you well again.

milk

Milk is a white liquid that mother animals make to feed their babies. Many people drink cows' milk.

map

A **map** is a drawing that shows you where places are so you can find your way around.

mirror

A **mirror** is a sheet of special glass that you can see yourself in.

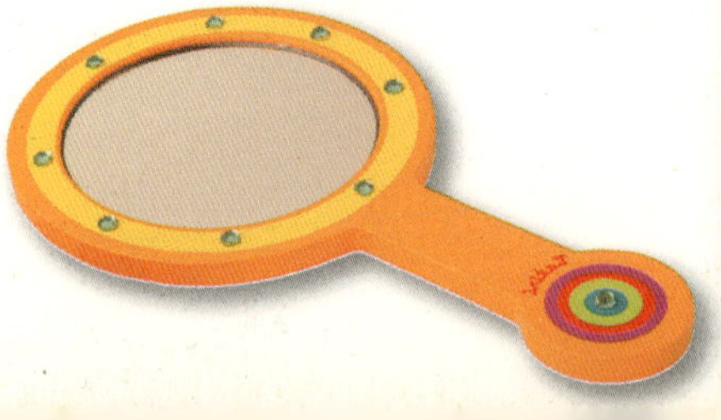

money

Money is the bills
and coins that
you use
o buy
hings.

mountain

A **mountain** is
a very tall piece
of land or rock.

moon

he **moon** shines
n the sky at night.
t is a big ball of rock
hat moves slowly
around the Earth
about once a month.

mouse

A **mouse** is a small,
furry animal with
a long tail. Mice have
sharp front teeth
for gnawing
food.

mushroom

A **mushroom** is a
living thing that looks
like a little umbrella.
You can eat some
mushrooms.

mug

A **mug** is a large,
straight cup with a
handle. You drink hot
drinks from
a mug.

music

Music is the sound
that people make
when they sing or
play instruments.

motorcycle

A **motorcycle** is a vehicle
with two wheels and
an engine.

Nn

needle

A **needle** is a thin, smooth piece of metal used for sewing. It is sharp at one end and has a hole for thread at the other.

net

A **net** is made from pieces of string or thread tied together with holes in between. Nets are used for catching fish and also in games such as tennis and soccer.

nose

Your **nose** is part of your face. You use it for breathing and smelling.

nurse

A **nurse** is a person who takes care of people who are sick or hurt. Nurses often work in hospitals.

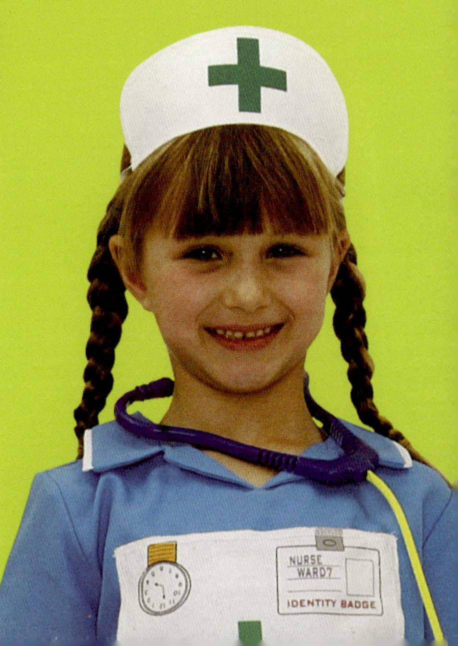

nest

A **nest** is the home that animals like birds and mice make for their babies.

number

A **number** tells you how many you have of something. 3 and 100 are numbers.

Oo

opposite

An **opposite** is completely different. The opposite of full is empty.

orange

An **orange** is a round, juicy fruit with orange-colored peel.

oven

An **oven** is the compartment in a stove where you roast or bake food.

owl

An **owl** is a bird that hunts for small animals at night. It has big eyes to help it see in the dark.

Pp

paint

Paint is a liquid that you put on to things to change the color.

paper

Paper is a very thin material used for drawing and writing.

parrot

A **parrot** is a bird with brightly colored feathers and a sharp, curved beak. Some parrots can talk.

penguin

Penguins are seabirds with black-and-white feathers that mostly live on cold, rocky coastlines. Penguins cannot fly but use their wings as flippers to swim.

pen

You use a **pen** to write or draw in ink.

pencil

A **pencil** is a long, thin stick of wood with black or colored lead in the middle. Pencils are used for writing and drawing.

pet

A **pet** is a tame animal that you take care of in your home. Dogs, cats, and hamsters are often kept as pets.

pig

A **pig** is an animal with a fat body, shor legs, and a curly tail.

pirate

A **pirate** is a sailor who attacks and robs other sailors at sea.

plate

A **plate** is a flat dish that you put food on.

pumpkin

A **pumpkin** is a large fruit with orange skin.

play

When you **play**, you have fun with your friends and join in games. Children and baby animals love to play with toys.

puppet

A **puppet** is a toy figure. You move a puppet by pulling strings or by putting your hand inside it.

plant

A **plant** is a living thing that grows in soil or water. Trees, flowers, and grass are all plants.

present

A **present** is something special that you give to someone to make them happy.

Qq

queen

A **queen** is a woman who is born to rule a country. A king's wife is also called a queen.

question

A **question** is what you ask when you want to know something.

Rr

rabbit

A **rabbit** is a small, furry animal with long ears and a fluffy tail.

rain

Rain is lots of little drops of water that fall from the clouds.

read

When you **read**, you understand words that are written down.

rhinoceros

A **rhinoceros** is a big animal with tough, leathery skin and horns on its head.

rainbow

A **rainbow** is an arch of bright colors that you see when the sun shines through rain.

robot

A **robot** is a machine that can do some of the jobs that people do.

Ss

sandwich

A **sandwich** is made of two slices of bread with a filling, such as cheese or ham, between them.

scissors

A pair of **scissors** is a tool used to cut paper or cloth. Scissors have two sharp blades and two handles.

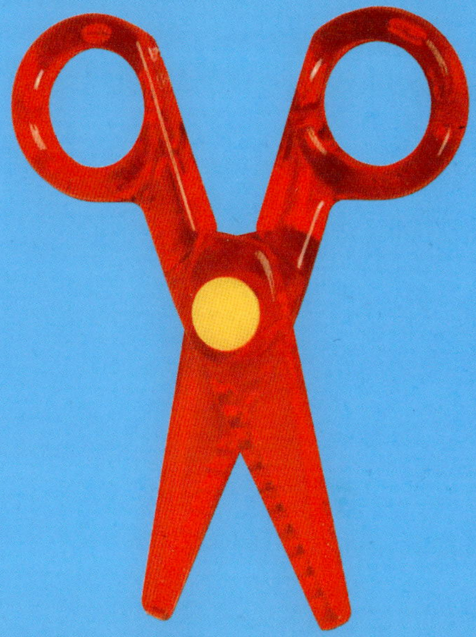

rocket

A **rocket** is the part of a spacecraft that pushes it high into space.

saucepan

A **saucepan** is a deep, metal cooking pot with a handle and usually a lid.

shape

The **shape** of something is its outline or the way it looks on the outside.

ruler

A **ruler** is a long, flat tool used for drawing lines and measuring length.

saw

A **saw** is a tool with sharp, metal teeth for cutting through wood.

shark

A **shark** is a big fish. Some sharks have very sharp teeth and can attack people.

snake

A **snake** has a long body and no legs. Its skin is made of scales.

sheep

A **sheep** is an animal with a thick, woolly coat. Male sheep are called rams, females are called ewes, and babies are called lambs.

shoe

You wear **shoes** on your feet to protect them.

snowman

A **snowman** is made out of snow and shaped like a person

sleep

When you **sleep**, you close your eyes and rest.

shell

A **shell** is a hard covering around something. Shellfish and nuts have shells.

smile

A **smile** is when the corners of your mouth turn up. You smile when you feel happy.

sock

You wear **socks** on your feet to keep them warm.

spade

A **spade** is a tool used to dig holes in the ground. It has a long handle and a flat, metal end.

strawberry

A **strawberry** is a soft, sweet, red fruit with seeds on it.

spider

A **spider** is an animal with eight legs. Spiders spin webs to catch insects for food.

squirrel

A **squirrel** is a small, furry animal that lives in trees. It has a bushy tail and eats nuts.

sun

The **Sun** shines in the sky and gives the Earth light and heat. It is a star and the Earth moves around it.

star

A **star** is a small, bright light in the sky. You can see stars on a clear, dark night. A star is also a shape with five or more points.

swan

A **swan** is a large bird with a long neck. It lives on rivers and lakes.

spoon

A **spoon** has a long handle and a round part at one end. You use a spoon to eat foods like soup and cereal.

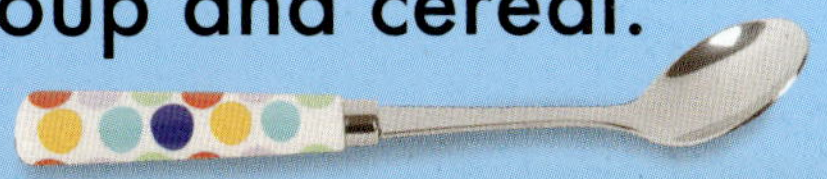

starfish

A **starfish** is an animal with five arms that lives in the ocean. It is shaped like a star.

Tt

table

A **table** is a piece of furniture with legs and a flat top. You can eat at a table.

telephone

A **telephone** is a machine you use to talk to someone in another place.

thermometer

You use a **thermometer** to fin out how hot or cold something is.

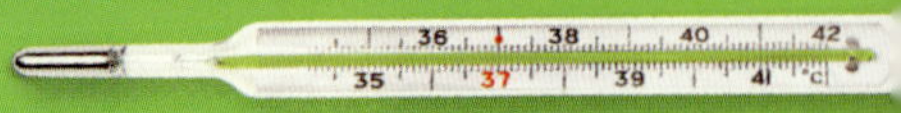

tail

An animal's **tail** grows at the end of its body. It helps the animal to balance.

tent

A **tent** is a shelter made out of a piece of cloth stretched over metal poles. You use a tent for camping.

tiger

A **tiger** is a big, wild cat with orange-and-black striped fur. Wild tigers are rare, but some still live in India and China.

tomato

A **tomato** is a soft, ed, round fruit that you often eat n salads.

towel

A **towel** is a piece of soft, thick cloth that you use to dry yourself.

tree

A **tree** is a tall plant with leaves, branches, and a thick stem of wood called a trunk.

ool

A **tool** is something you hold in your hands to help you do things. Wrenches, saws, and hammers are all tools.

toy

A **toy** is something a child plays with. Dolls, kites, teddy bears, and train sets are all toys.

truck

A **truck** is a strong vehicle that takes things from one place to another.

toothbrush

You use a **toothbrush** and toothpaste to keep your teeth clean.

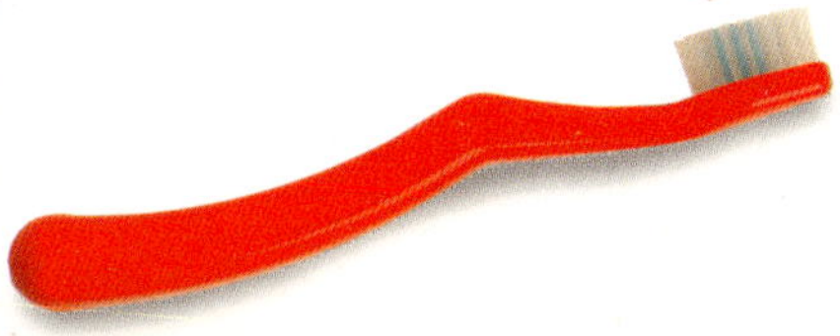

tractor

A **tractor** is a farm vehicle with big back wheels to pull things.

Uu

umbrella

An **umbrella** keeps you dry when it rains.

uniform

Some people wear a **uniform** to show what job they do or which school they go to.

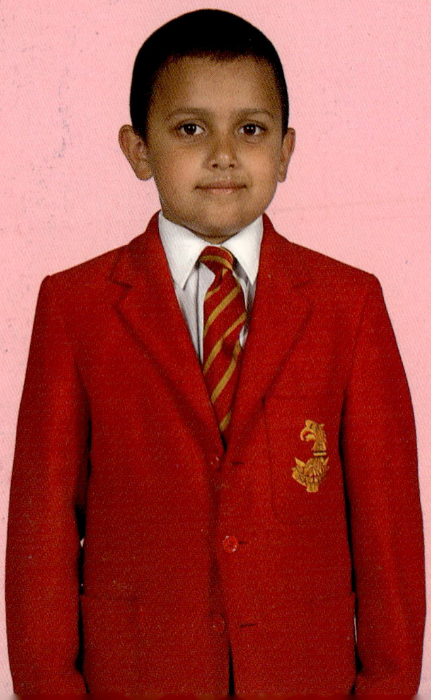

Vv

vacuum cleaner

A **vacuum cleaner** is a machine that sucks up dust and dirt.

vase

A **vase** is a kind of container you can use to hold cut flowers in water.

vegetable

A **vegetable** is a plant that can be eaten raw or cooked. Carrots, cabbages, and onions are all vegetables.

violin

A **violin** is a musical instrument made of wood. You play it using a bow.

Ww

watch

A **watch** is a small clock that you can wear on your wrist. It tells you what time it is.

wheel

Wheels are round and they can turn. Bicycles, cars, and trains all have wheels so that they can move.

water

Water is a clear liquid found in rivers, lakes, and oceans. Water also comes out of faucets.

woman

A **woman** is a grown-up female person.

Xx

X-ray

An **X-ray** is a picture that lets a doctor see inside your body.

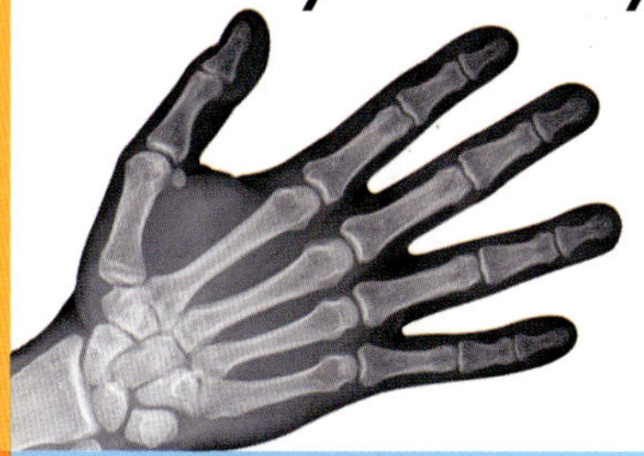

xylophone

A **xylophone** is a musical instrument with a row of wooden bars.

Yy

yogurt

Yogurt is a food made from milk. It is often mixed with fruit.

yacht

A **yacht** is a boat with sails or an engine. Yachts are used for fun.

yolk

The **yolk** is the middle part of an egg.

yo-yo

A **yo-yo** is a round toy that you roll up and down on a string.

yawn

When you **yawn**, you open your mouth wide and breathe out noisily.

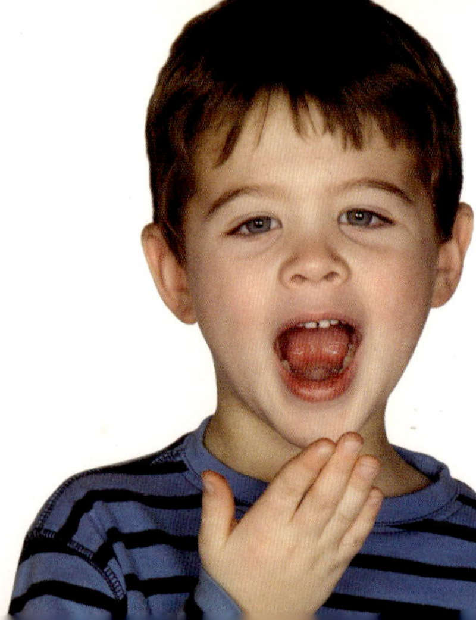

Zz

zebra

A **zebra** looks like a horse with black-and-white stripes. Zebras live in Africa

zipper

A **zipper** joins two pieces of material together. The zipper teeth lock together when you close it.

FIRST dictionary

Thematic pages

Wild animals

Animals are known as **wild animals** if they move around freely in the oceans, in the air, or on the land.

snake

frog

eagle

crocodile

shark

tiger

elephant

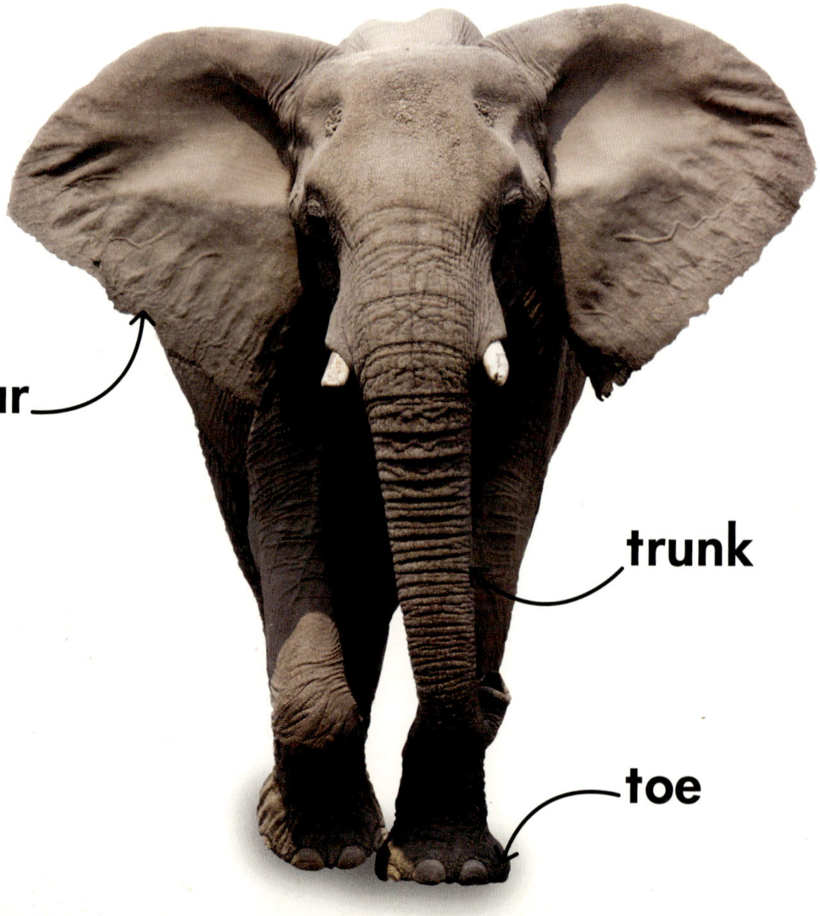

Farm animals

People keep **farm animals** for food such as meat or milk, and for their skin or fur.

rooster

pig

goat

chick

sheep

cows

Pets

A **pet** is a tame animal, such as a dog or a hamster, that you care for, often in your home or yard.

dog

pony

cat

hamster

goldfish

rabbit

macaw

guinea pig

Birds

A **bird** is an animal with wings, feathers, and a beak. Most birds are able to fly.

finch

owl

eagle

swan

hornbill

pigeon

ostrich

penguins

Insects

An **insect** is a small animal with six legs. An insect's body is divided into three parts. Some insects have wings.

bee

fly

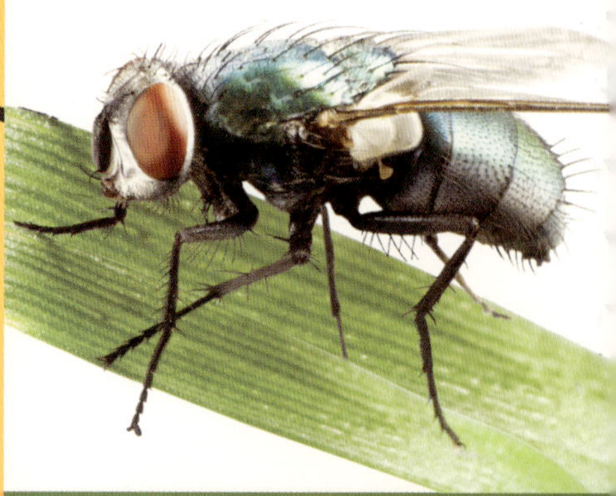

butterflies

wasp

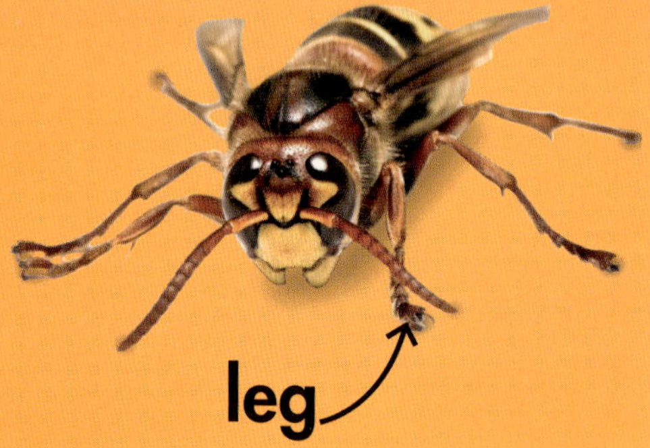

ant

dragonfly

grasshopper

ladybug

Food

Food is anything that you eat to help you grow and keep you healthy. Cheese, vegetables, fruit, and bread are all food.

sandwich

pasta

pie

carrots

cupcake

nuts

sausages

bread

cheese

banana

Fruit

A **fruit** is the part of a plant that holds the seeds. Many fruits are juicy and delicious to eat.

grapes

watermelon

pineapple

starfruit

apple

strawberry

banana

peach

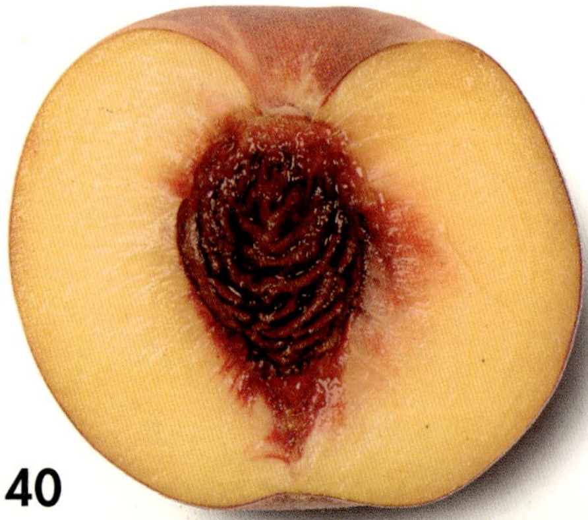

tomato

raspberry

Vegetables

A **vegetable** is the part of a plant that is used for food. Beans, cabbages, cauliflowers, onions, potatoes, and peas are all vegetables.

leek

cabbage

pepper

onion

broccoli

peas

corn

potato

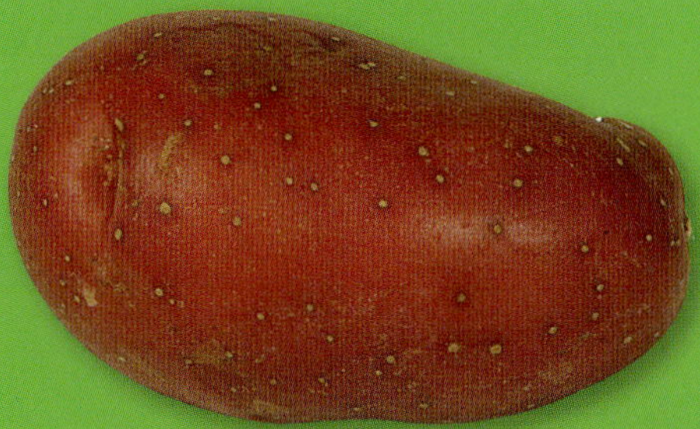

beans

cauliflower

Face

Your **face** is the front part of your head. Your eyes, nose, and mouth are all parts of your face.

Clothes

Clothes are things
hat people wear.
Socks, shoes, pants,
hirts, and hats are
all clothes.

hat

gloves

boots

underpants

shirt

horts

pajamas

scarf

dress

shoes

Family

A **family** is a group of people who are related to each other. Most families have parents, children, and grandchildren.

mother

sisters

grandfather

aunt

grandmother

brothers

cousins

father

Garden

A **garden** is where people grow flowers and vegetables. A person's garden is usually next to his or her house.

ant

watering can

acorn

flower

trowel

spider

tree

frog

boots

Toys

A **toy** is something you play with. Dolls, teddy bears, kites, train sets, and jigsaw puzzles are all toys.

tricycle

doll

jigsaw puzzle

train

balloons

ball

teddy bears

dinosaur

bat

kite

blocks

Tools

A **tool** is something you use to help you do a job. Hammers, screwdrivers, saws, drills, and wrenches are all tools.

drill

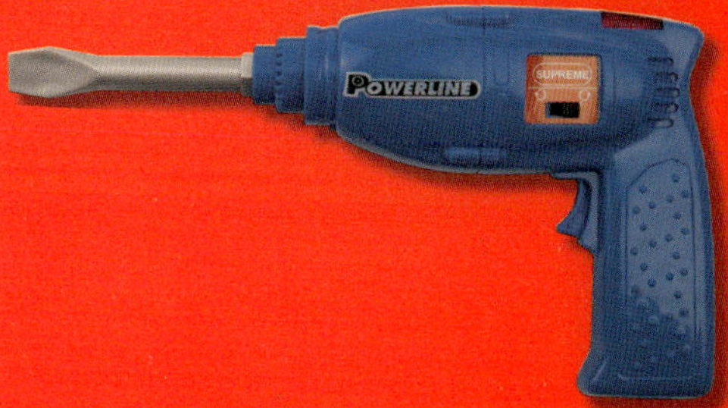

wrenches

scissors

screwdrivers

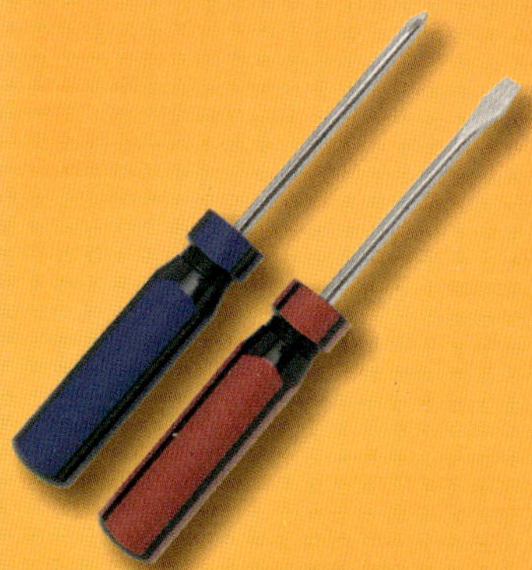

watering can

hammer

pliers

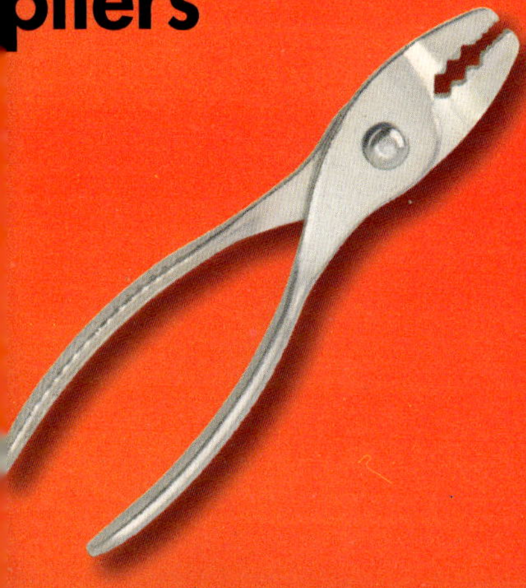

trowel

tool box

School

School is the place you go to learn. At school, teachers teach children how to read, write, count, and other important things.

teacher

glue

books

triangle

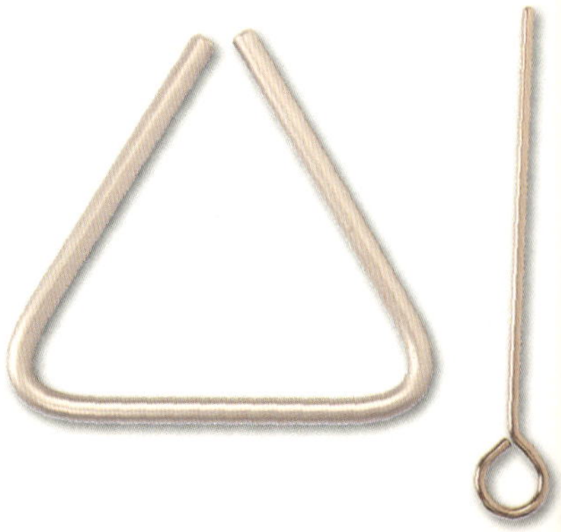

violin

ruler

paints

paper

pen

brushes

tambourine

Beach

A **beach** is the strip of land on the edge of the ocean. Beaches are usually covered with sand or pebbles.

sandcastle

bucket

spade

deckchair

swimsuit

pinwheel

starfish

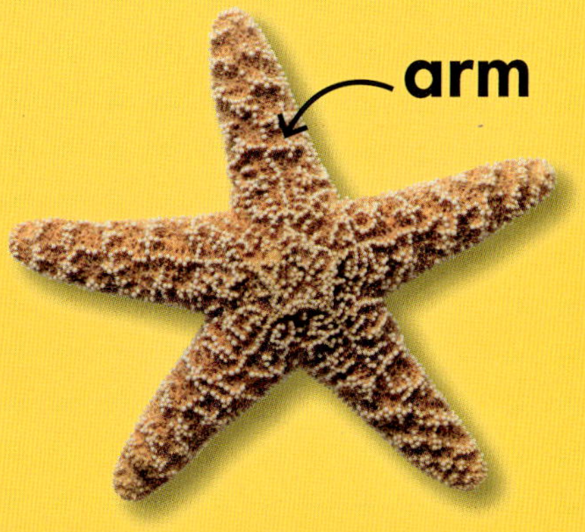

arm

shell

boat

Things that go

Trucks, trains, buses, and cars carry people and goods on land. Boats travel on the water and planes fly through the air.

truck

helicopter

blade

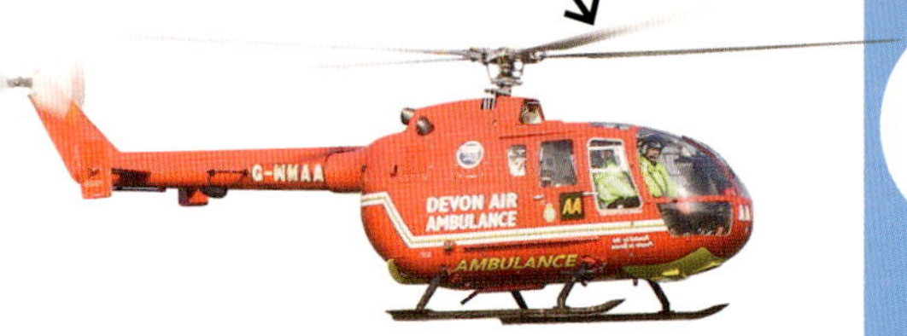

car

scooter

hot-air balloon

basket

tractor

airplane

ambulance

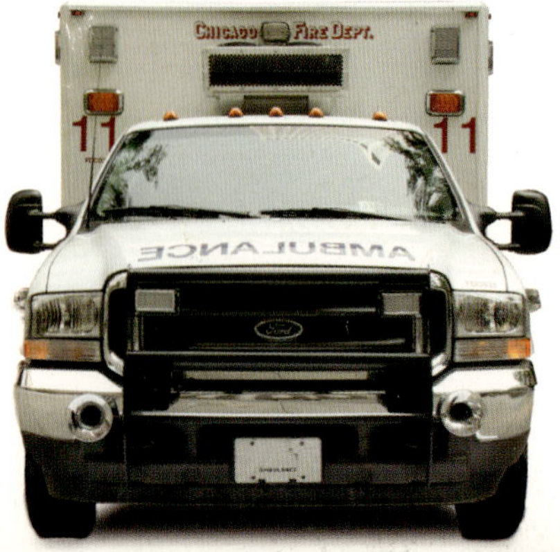

bicycle

quad bike

rocket

bus

train

boat

motorcycle

bulldozer

van

dumper

fire truck

Doing words

Words that describe what we are doing are known as verbs. Most verbs describe actions, such as eating, drinking, reading, or jumping.

hopping

skipping

crouching

bathing

swinging

walking

hugging

yawning

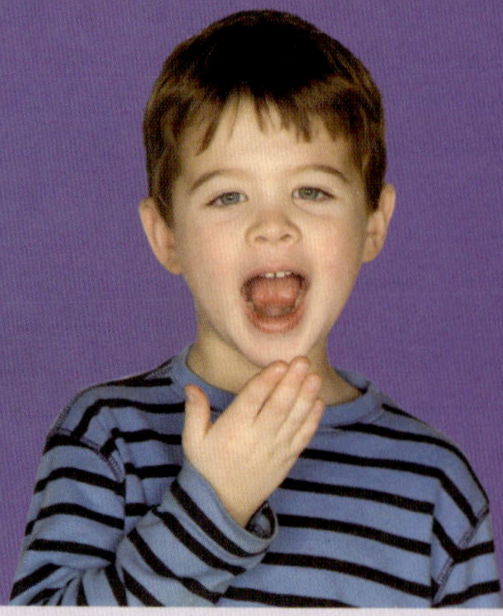

kissing

catching

crawling

Time

Time is measured in minutes, hours, days, weeks, months, and years. The time is a particular moment in the day.

Days of the week

Sunday

Monday

Tuesday

Wednesday

Thursday

Friday

Saturday

Months

January

February

March

April

May

June

July

August

September

October

November

December

four o'clock

quarter past four

half past four

quarter to five

Seasons

spring

summer

fall

winter

Shapes

A **shape** is the way an object looks on the outside, or the pattern you make when you draw around it. Circles, squares, and triangles are shapes.

circle

star

heart

rectangle

triangle

cheese

square

pentagon

spiral

cylinder

sphere

cube

Colors

Red, yellow, and blue are **colors**. By mixing them together you can make other colors, such as green, purple, and orange.

black

blue

red

yellow

green

brown

gray

orange

white

purple

pink

Opposites

When things are the **opposite** of each other, they are completely different. Tall is the opposite of short and hot is the opposite of cold.

awake

asleep

light

dark

big

little

hot

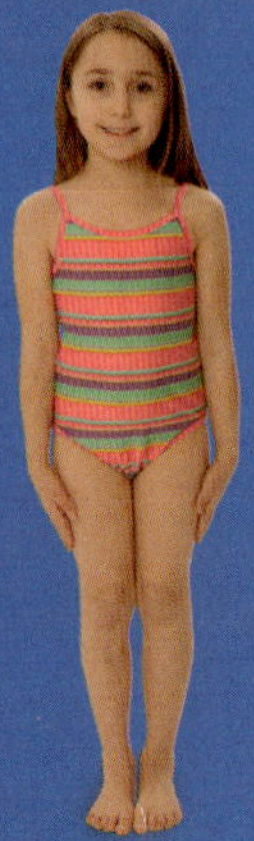

cold

dirty

clean

dry

baby

wet

full
empty
thin
fat
tall
fast
hare
slow
snail
tortoise
old
new
open
short
shut
happy
sad

Numbers

Numbers tell you how many people or things there are. A number can be written as a word (one, two, three) or as a numeral (1, 2, 3).

1 one frog

2 two babies

6 six tractors

7 seven puppi

20 twenty cupcakes

50 fifty jelly beans

3 three kittens

4 four wrenches

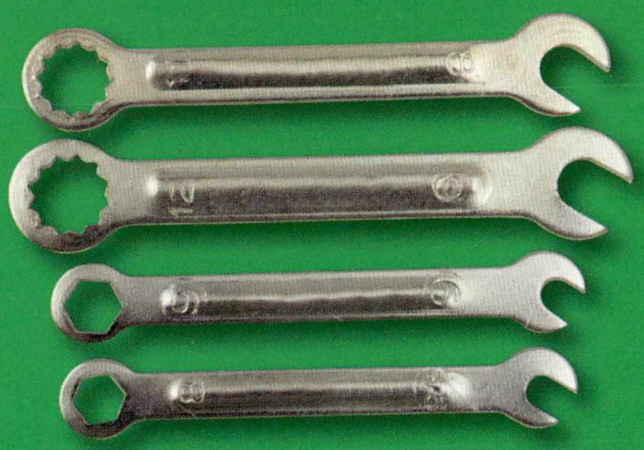

5 five tomatoes

8 eight flowers

9 nine ducklings

10 ten paints

100 one hundred buttons